When You Were Young

When You Were Young

A Memory Book for the First Two Years

Illustrated by Emily Boland

Abbeville Press • Publishers
New York • London • Paris

When You Were Young was specially designed for you to record feelings, thoughts, and important events during your child's first two years. Throughout the book, passages intended for a specific parent are marked [Mother] or [Father], inviting you both to participate in creating this original keepsake for your child.

Art director: James Wageman
Designer: Renée Khatami
Editor: Alison Mitchell
Production manager: Dana Cole

First edition, ninth printing.

Printed and bound by Toppan Printing Co., Japan.

A Jane Lahr/Promised Land Production

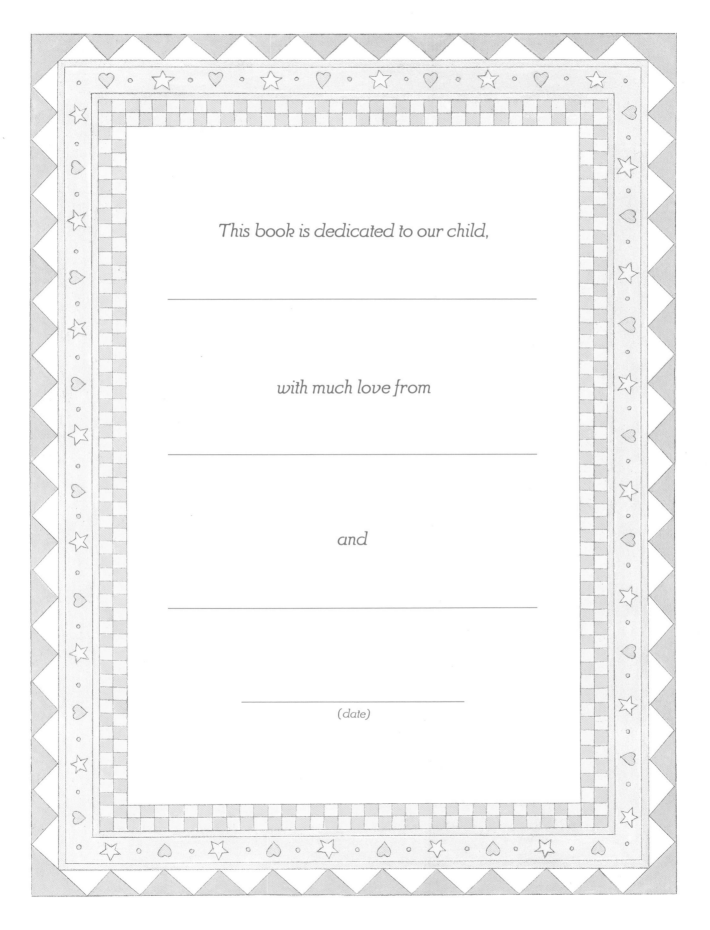

This book is dedicated to our child,

_____

with much love from

_____

and

_____

_____
(date)

CONTENTS

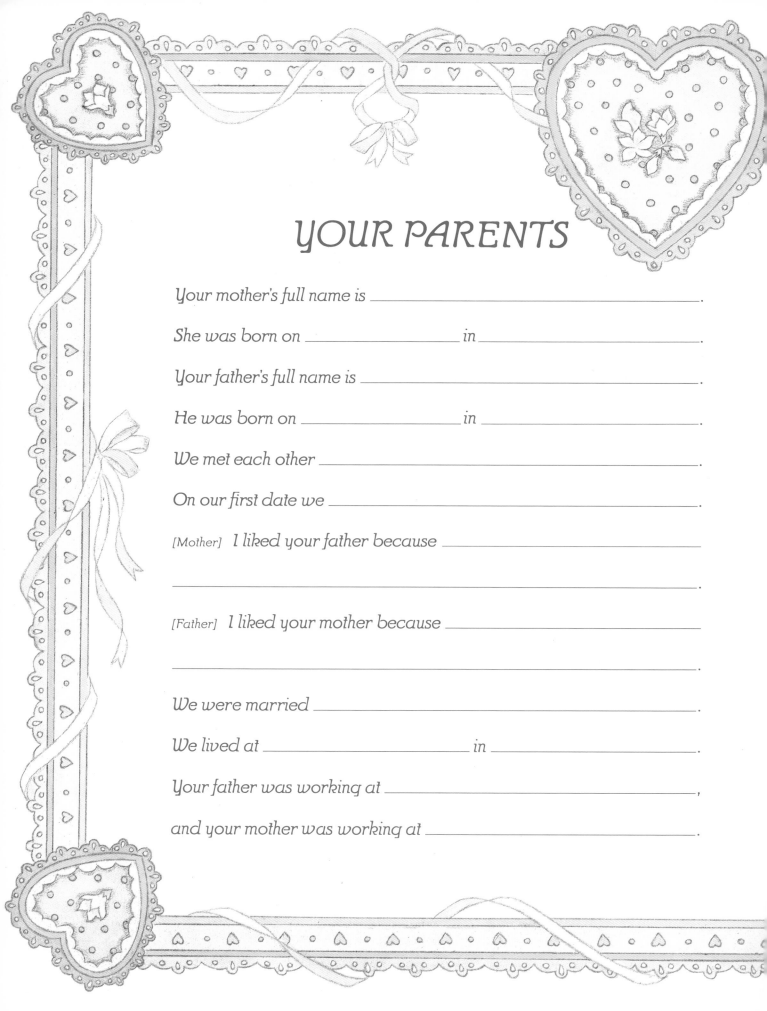

YOUR PARENTS

Your mother's full name is _____.

She was born on _____ in _____.

Your father's full name is _____.

He was born on _____ in _____.

We met each other _____.

On our first date we _____.

[Mother] I liked your father because _____

_____.

[Father] I liked your mother because _____

_____.

We were married _____.

We lived at _____ in _____.

Your father was working at _____,

and your mother was working at _____.

[This is how we looked.]

Before you came into our life, we used to spend our time _____

_____

_____.

Some of our closest friends were _____

_____.

For fun, we liked to _____

_____.

We especially wanted a child because _____

_____

_____.

9

Your Mother's
Family Tree

Your Father's
Family Tree

COMING INTO THE WORLD

We first found out I was pregnant on

_____, and celebrated the news by

_____.

I loved being pregnant because _____

_____.

[Mother] I first heard your heartbeat _____,

and felt you kicking _____.

[Father] I first heard your heartbeat _____,

and felt you kicking _____.

[I looked like this when I was pregnant with you.]

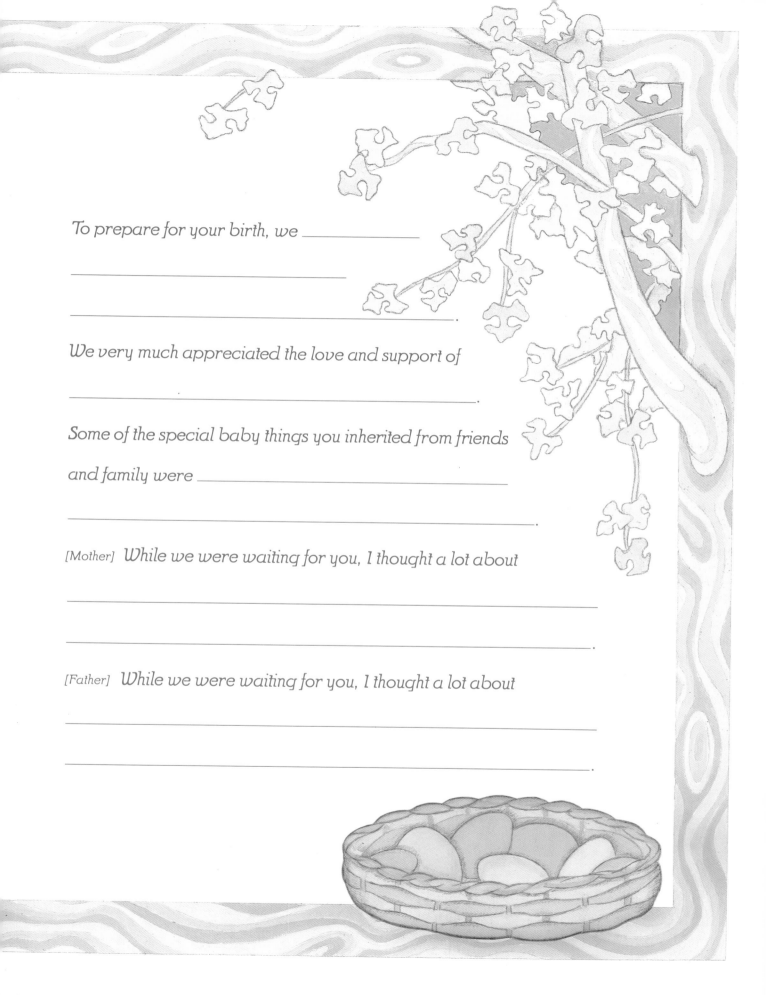

To prepare for your birth, we _____

_____

_____.

We very much appreciated the love and support of

_____.

Some of the special baby things you inherited from friends

and family were _____

_____.

[Mother] While we were waiting for you, I thought a lot about

_____

_____.

[Father] While we were waiting for you, I thought a lot about

_____

_____.

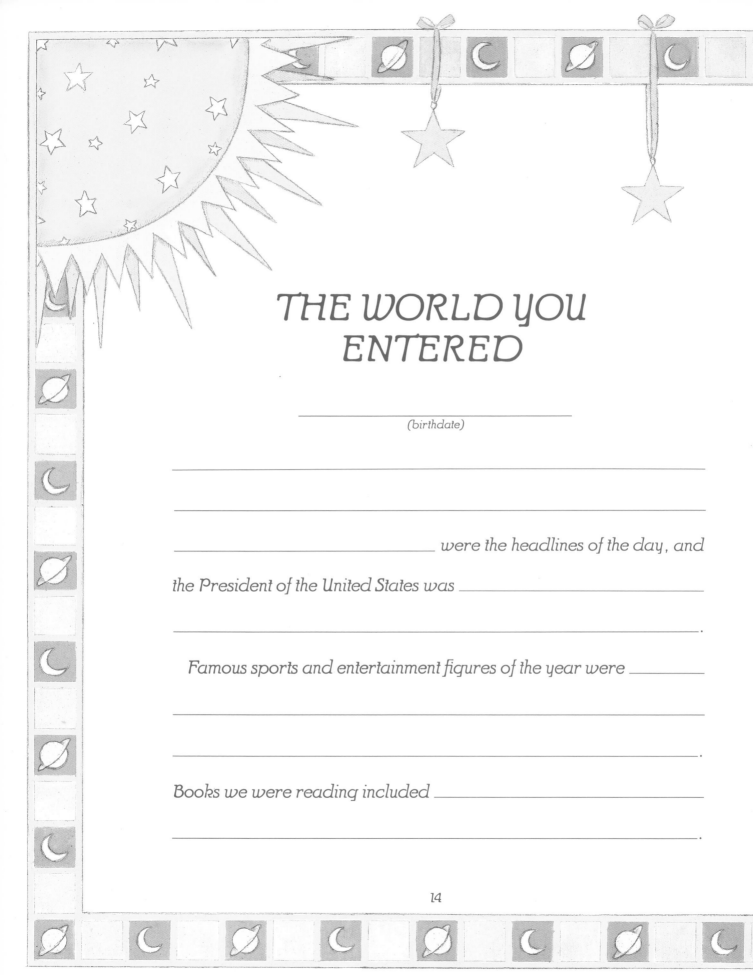

THE WORLD YOU ENTERED

_____

(birthdate)

_____

_____

_____ were the headlines of the day, and

the President of the United States was _____

_____.

Famous sports and entertainment figures of the year were _____

_____

_____.

Books we were reading included _____

_____.

Our favorite movie was _____

and starred _____ .

We listened to music by _____

_____ ,

and _____ was the latest fad.

   This year, people were talking a lot about _____

_____

_____ .

In addition to your birth, these events made the year special:

_____

_____

_____

_____ .

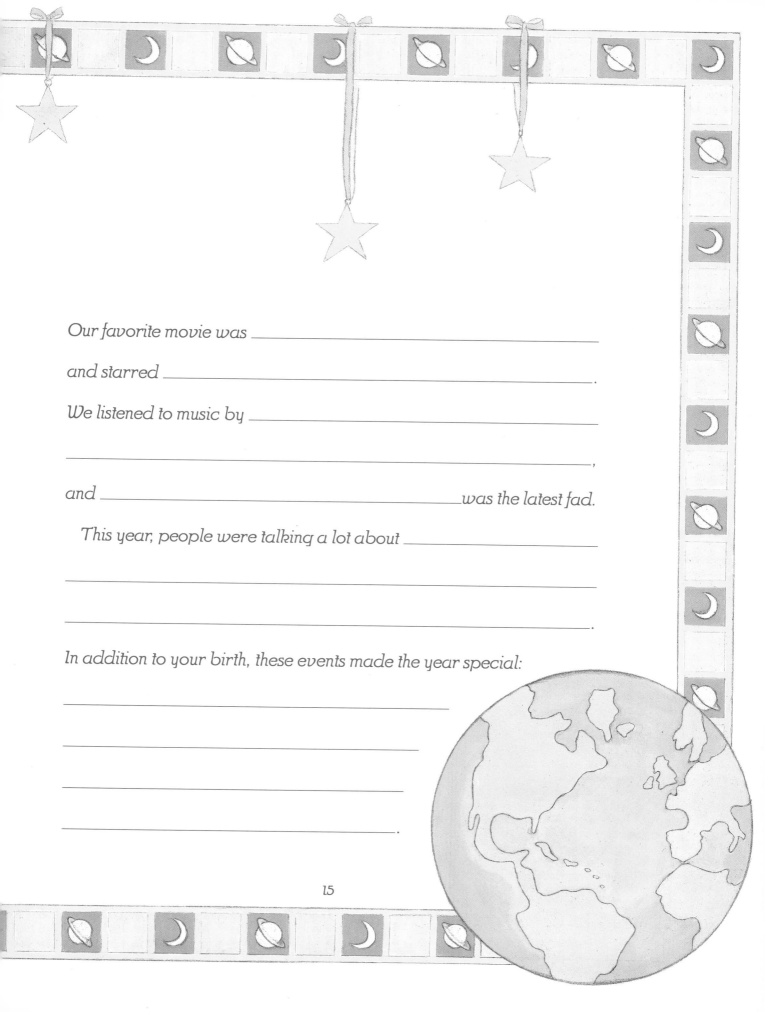

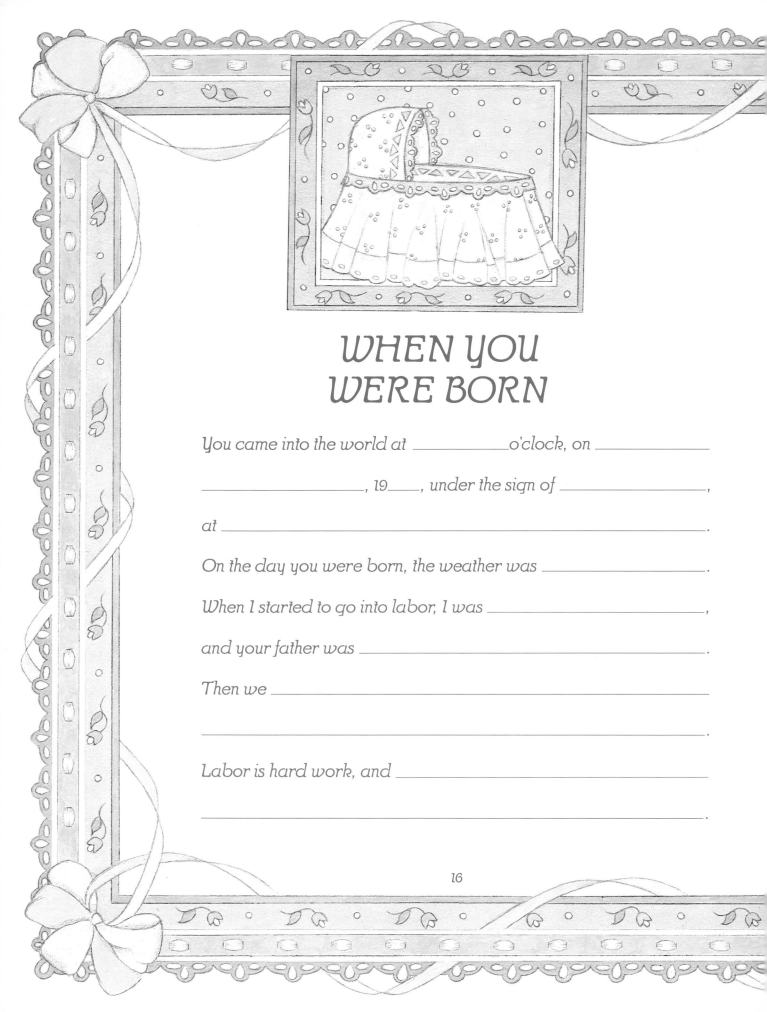

WHEN YOU WERE BORN

You came into the world at _____ o'clock, on _____

_____, 19_____, under the sign of _____,

at _____.

On the day you were born, the weather was _____.

When I started to go into labor, I was _____,

and your father was _____.

Then we _____

_____.

Labor is hard work, and _____

_____.

While your mother was in labor, I _____

_____ .

_____ and _____ helped to deliver you.

Present at your birth were _____

_____ .

[Mother] When I first saw you, I felt _____

_____

_____

_____ .

[Father] When I first saw you, I felt _____

_____

_____

_____ .

You weighed _____ pounds, _____ ounces, and you were

_____ inches long. You had _____ hair, and

your eyes were _____ .

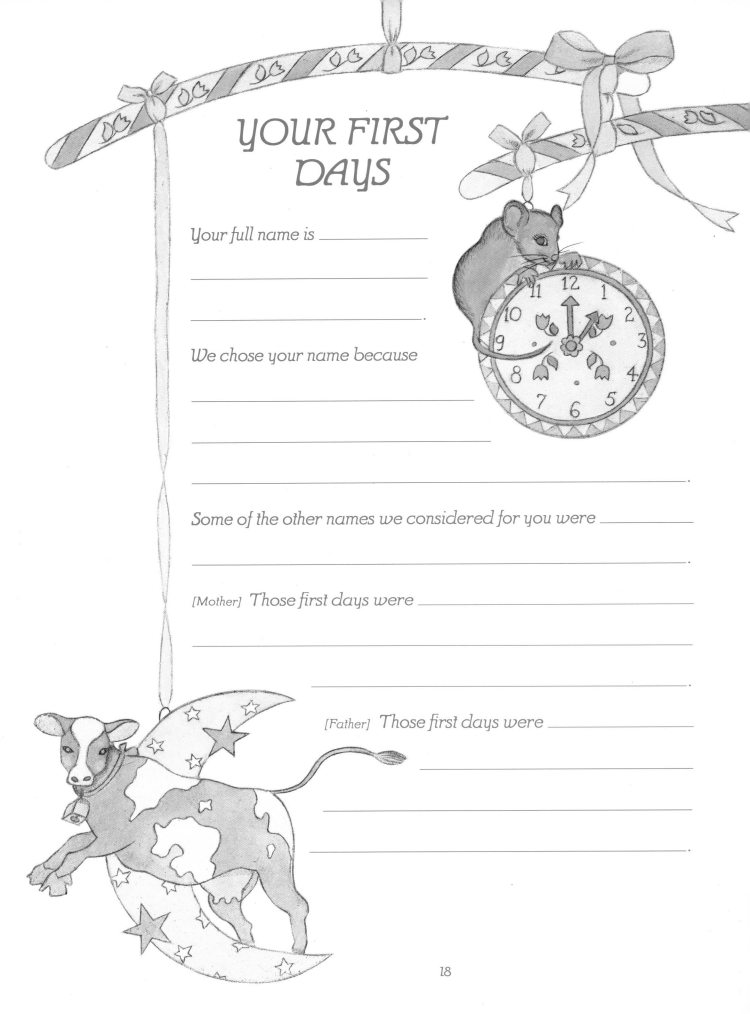

YOUR FIRST DAYS

Your full name is _____

_____

_____ .

We chose your name because _____

_____

_____ .

Some of the other names we considered for you were _____

_____ .

[Mother] Those first days were _____

_____

_____ .

[Father] Those first days were _____

_____

_____ .

[Here is a photograph taken soon after you were born.]

Our first visitors were _____

_____.

When the family first saw you, they said:

_____ : _____

_____

_____ : _____

_____

_____ : _____

_____

_____ : _____

_____

BRINGING YOU HOME

We brought you home to _____

_____ on _____.

Waiting to welcome you were _____

_____.

The special place we had prepared for you was _____

_____.

During the first few weeks _____

helped us take care of you.

We announced your arrival to the world:

[announcement]

Gifts:

Giver _____   *Gift* _____

_____   _____

_____   _____

_____   _____

_____   _____

_____   _____

_____   _____

Celebrations and ceremonies:

_____

_____

_____

_____

YOUR FIRST THREE MONTHS

During your first three months you slept in a

_____ in _____ room.

At first you slept about _____ hours at a time,

then _____ hours, and when you were

_____ weeks old, you slept through the night.

We fed you _____,

about _____ times a day and _____ at night.

By the time you were three months old, you weighed _____ pounds,

_____ ounces, and had grown to _____ inches in length.

[Mother] When you woke up at night, I would _____

_____. When you cried or were upset, I comforted you

by _____.

[Father] When you woke up at night, I would _____

_____. When you cried or were upset, I comforted you

by _____.

You first smiled when you were _____ old; you were smiling at

_____.

You lifted your head by yourself when you were _____ weeks old, and though you didn't know how to talk yet, you started to coo and gurgle _____ weeks after you were born.

You were growing every day, and we noticed _____

_____

_____

_____

[Mother] This time was _____

_____

_____

[Father] This time was _____

_____

_____

YOUR SECOND
THREE MONTHS

You started reaching out for the world around you in these ways:

_____

(age)

_____   _____

_____   _____

_____   _____

We loved watching you respond to new experiences. Your face

expressed _____

_____.

[Mother] *We worked as a team to take care of you. I usually* _____

_____,

[Father] *and I usually* _____

_____.

We took turns _____

_____.

Your bath was always a special event, and _____

_____.

Other people who were a part of your life were _____

_____.

When we went out on errands, you seemed to like _____

_____.

The season was _____,

and we_____.

[Mother] One of my favorite memories of you at this age is _____

_____

_____.

[Father] One of my favorite memories of you at this age is _____

_____

_____.

ON THE WAY
TO ONE

What was extraordinary about you as you grew was _____

_____

_____

_____.

We watched you change as you learned to _____

at age _____, _____ at age _____,

_____ at age _____, and _____

_____ when you were _____.

When we went for walks, you came along in a _____.

[Mother] I especially liked to take you _____

_____.

[Father] I especially liked to take you _____

_____.

The world was your oyster, and you liked exploring _____

_____.

You seemed particularly fascinated by _____

_____.

On the weekend, we often _____

_____.

[Mother] Parents often daydream about the future. Here are some of

my wishes for the world in which you'll be growing up:_____

_____

_____

_____.

[Father] Here are some of my wishes for the world in which you'll be

growing up: _____

_____

_____.

A YEAR OF GROWING

Imagine that in one year you grew from _____ pounds,

_____ ounces, and _____ inches long to _____

pounds, _____ ounces, and _____ inches!

What most surprised us about you was _____

_____

_____.

You made us laugh when _____

_____.

We really worried when _____

_____.

You got your first haircut on _____.

You looked very _____.

Here is a lock of your hair:

Other people who looked after you this year were _____

_____

_____.

[Mother] Being with you has changed me in these ways: _____

_____

_____.

[Father] Being with you has changed me in these ways: _____

_____

_____.

Together, we learned _____

_____.

Because of you, we feel _____

_____.

Other important changes for us this year were _____

_____.

YOUR FAVORITES

During your first year, your favorite foods were _____

_____

_____.

When you went to sleep, you liked to have your _____

_____ with you.

Your most beloved toys were _____

_____,

and you were drawn to things that were _____ in color.

Games we used to play with you were _____

_____

_____.

The music you responded to was _____

_____

_____.

With your mother, you especially liked to _____

_____

_____.

With your father, you especially liked to _____

_____

_____.

Some other people who were special friends of yours were _____

_____.

Here are some of your other favorites: _____

_____

_____

_____.

What you liked least of all was _____

_____

_____.

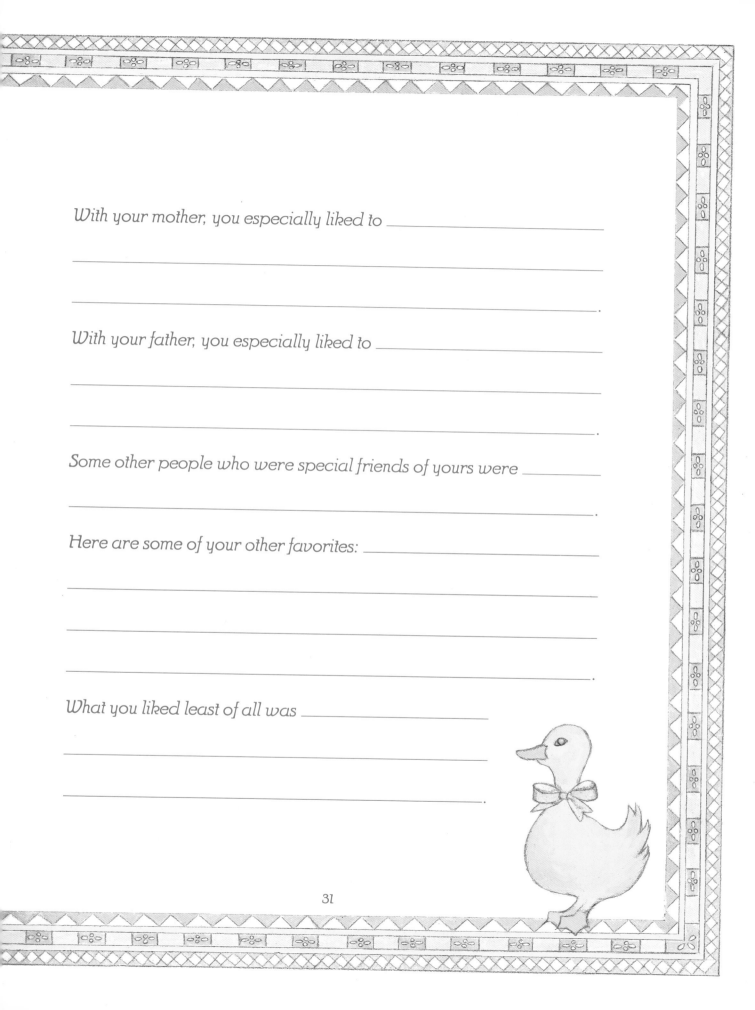

Date:

Place:

Time:

YOUR FIRST BIRTHDAY PARTY

We celebrated your birthday by _____

_____.

You wore _____,

and the cake was a _____.

Special gifts you received were

_____ from _____,

_____ from _____,

_____ from _____,

and _____ from _____.

At the party, you most enjoyed _____

_____.

[This is how we all looked.]

Guests:

_____

_____

_____

_____

_____

This day was special for all of us because _____

_____

_____

_____

_____

FAMILY GATHERINGS

HOLIDAYS

For your first _____, we gathered at

_____. The guests

were _____

_____.

The tradition that captured your attention was _____

_____.

On _____, we all got together at

_____. Staying for dinner were

_____.

The highlight of your day was _____

_____.

We celebrated _____ by _____

_____.

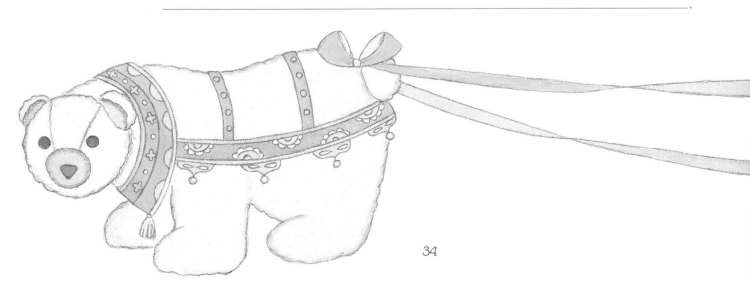

We'll never forget _____

_____.

For your first _____, we went to

_____, and _____

_____.

PARTIES

Date: _____ Guests: _____

_____.

The festivities included _____

_____

_____.

Date: _____ Guests: _____

_____.

You had fun _____

_____.

FAMILY OUTINGS

We first went to visit relatives, your _____,

on _____ for _____.

We traveled there by _____.

You had a wonderful time _____

_____.

We visited your _____ on _____,

and _____.

What you liked most there was _____

_____.

Your first _____ trip was to _____,

where we _____

_____

_____.

Other jaunts this year: _____

_____

_____.

Your favorite outing seemed to be _____,

because _____

_____.

[Mother] An adventure I particularly enjoyed was _____

_____,

because _____

_____.

[Father] An adventure I particularly enjoyed was _____

_____,

because _____

_____.

WHAT YOUR DAY
WAS LIKE

We knew you were awake when _____

_____

_____ .

You got up most mornings at _____ o'clock.

For breakfast, you usually ate _____

_____ , and

during the morning, you often _____

_____ .

At lunchtime, _____

_____

_____ .

Indoors, you entertained yourself by _____

_____

_____ .

When you went outside, you loved to _____

_____

_____ .

Afternoons were your time to _____

_____ .

In the bath, you loved to _____

_____ .

You ate supper at _____ o'clock and then you usually

_____ .

When we put you to bed, you liked _____

_____

_____ ,

and you went to sleep after we _____

_____

_____ .

YOUR
MOTHER'S DAY

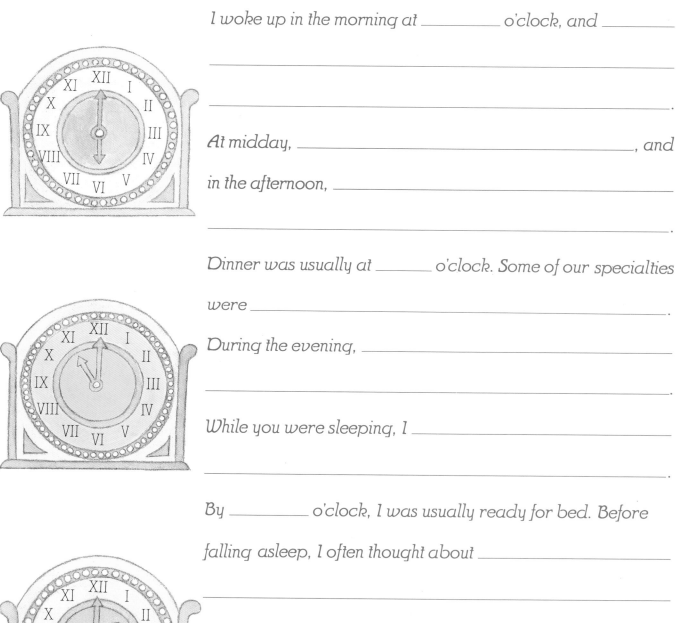

I woke up in the morning at _____ o'clock, and _____

_____

_____ .

At midday, _____ , and

in the afternoon, _____

_____ .

Dinner was usually at _____ o'clock. Some of our specialties

were _____ .

During the evening, _____

_____ .

While you were sleeping, I _____

_____ .

By _____ o'clock, I was usually ready for bed. Before

falling asleep, I often thought about _____

_____

_____ .

YOUR FATHER'S DAY

I woke up in the morning at _____ o'clock, and _____

_____

_____.

At midday, _____, and

in the afternoon, _____

_____.

Dinner was usually at _____ o'clock. Some of our specialties

were _____.

During the evening, _____

_____.

While you were sleeping, I _____

_____.

By _____ o'clock, I was usually ready for bed. Before

falling asleep, I often thought about _____

_____

_____.

WONDERFUL
YOU

Friends and family were always impressed by _____

_____

_____.

You had a way of _____

_____

_____

_____.

You showed your sense of humor by _____

_____.

Almost always, _____

_____ made you laugh.

When you felt loving, you _____

_____.

When you felt frustrated, you _____

_____.

You _____

_____ to get our attention.

When you were excited about something, you _____

_____

_____.

ACCOMPLISHMENTS

You took your first step _____ , *and*

you were heading toward _____ .

Before you spoke your first words, you had your own language that

sounded like: _____

_____ .

Your very first word was _____ , *and*

the next few words you learned were _____

_____

_____ .

Later, when you were _____ , *your first real sentence was*

_____

_____ .

You first fed yourself when you were _____, and you were

eating _____.

You helped us dress you when _____

_____.

You drew your first picture on _____.

It looked like _____.

Other landmarks and accomplishments that were yours:

_____

_____

_____

_____

_____

_____.

BEDTIME STORIES

The first book we read to you was _____

_____ by _____.

When you were very little, your favorite story was _____

_____.

We read it to you about _____ times a week.

You liked stories about _____

_____

and pictures of _____.

[Mother] When I was a child, some of my favorite stories were

_____

_____.

[Father] When I was a child, some of my favorite stories were

_____

_____.

Here are some other rhymes and stories you liked, and the people who recited them.

_____   _____
(story)   (teller)

_____   _____

_____   _____

_____   _____

You started turning pages and "reading" when you were

_____ months old.

The book you knew best was _____

_____.

After you were a year old, your favorite story was

_____

_____,

because _____

_____.

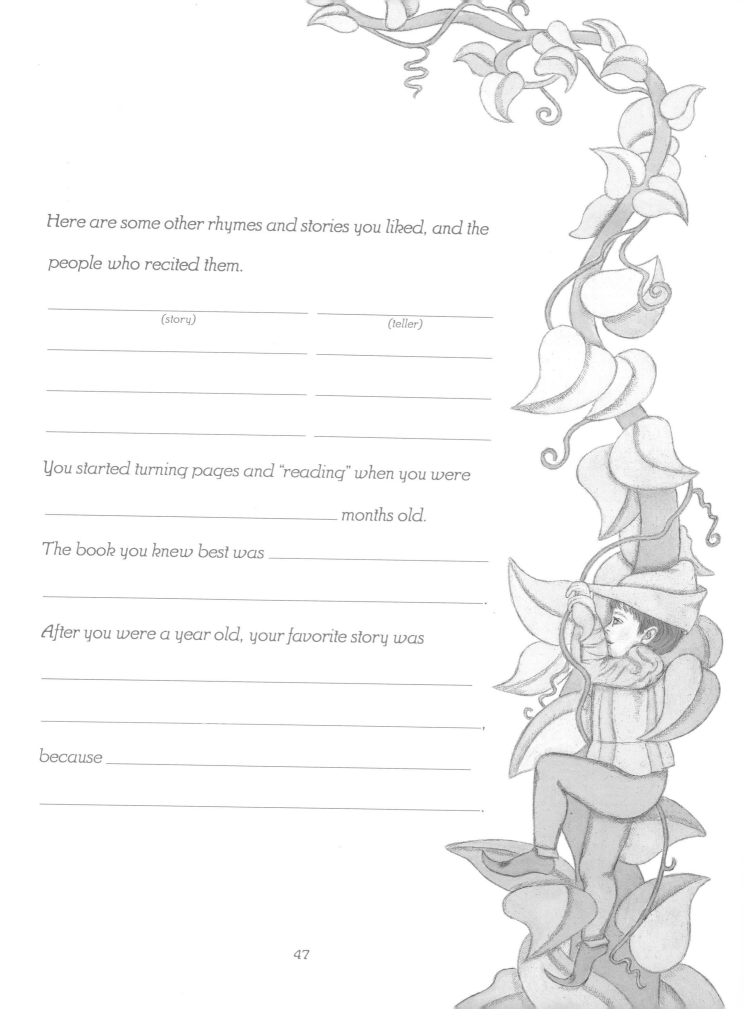

SECOND–YEAR FAVORITES

Your favorite foods after you were a year old were _____

_____

_____

_____.

You liked wearing your _____

_____,and hated wearing

_____.

The stuffed animal you loved most was _____,

and was named _____.

Your favorite song was _____

_____.

_____

_____ were your most beloved toys.

Your favorite activity was _____

_____,

and your least favorite was _____

_____.

With your mother, you especially liked to _____

_____

_____.

With your father, you especially liked to _____

_____

_____.

BEST FRIENDS

You began to play with friends when you were _____ months old.

Your friends were _____

_____

_____.

Your group used to _____

_____

_____

_____.

Your friends had birthdays, too, and during your first year you went

to the following parties:

_____   _____
(date)   (for whom)

You wore _____.

Your gift was _____.

_____   _____
(date)   (for whom)

You wore _____ .

Your gift was _____ .

_____   _____
(date)   (for whom)

You wore _____ .

Your gift was _____ .

Within our family, you enjoyed playing with _____

_____

_____

_____

_____ .

Your first four-legged friend was _____ ,

who belonged to _____ .

FIRST TWELVE MONTHS

[Photographs]

YEARS
ONE TO TWO

[Photographs]

A YEAR OF FAMILY FESTIVITIES

[Photographs]

FAMILY HISTORY AND RESEMBLANCES

Your mother's family is of _____ descent, and

has lived in this country for _____ generations.

Among your illustrious ancestors were _____

_____.

Some of the family traits and talents are _____

_____.

Your father's family is of _____ descent, and

has lived in this country for _____ generations.

Among your illustrious ancestors were _____

_____.

Some of the family traits and talents are _____

_____.

You share the color of your eyes with _____,

and the color of your hair with _____.

[Mother] You remind me of myself when you _____

_____.

You remind me of your father when you _____

_____.

[Father] You remind me of myself when you _____

_____.

You remind me of your mother when you _____

_____.

Other family resemblances we've noticed: _____

_____.

Date:

Place:

Time:

YOUR SECOND
BIRTHDAY PARTY

We celebrated your second birthday by _____

_____

_____ .

You wore _____ ,

and the cake was a _____ .

Special gifts you received were

_____ from _____ ,

_____ from _____ ,

_____ from _____ ,

and _____ from _____ .

[This is how we all looked.]

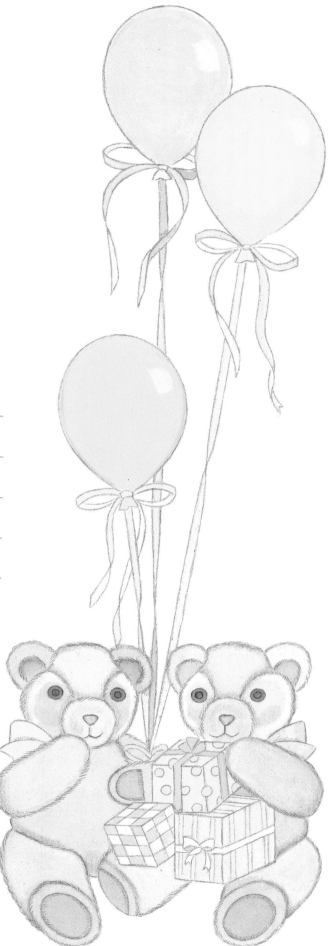

Guests:

_____

_____

_____

_____

_____

At the party, you most enjoyed

_____

_____

_____

_____

HIGHLIGHTING OUR YEAR

High points in our family life this year were _____

_____

_____

_____.

Landmarks in our work included _____

_____

_____.

Other milestones of the year : _____

_____

_____

_____.

We took you to _____ for the first time,

and _____

_____ .

[Mother] This year, I began to think about _____

_____

_____ .

[Father] This year, I began to think about _____

_____

_____ .

Some of the plans we made for our future included _____

_____

_____

_____ .

FOR YOU

[Mother] Here are some things I'd like you to know about how

I feel now: _____

_____

_____

_____

_____

Here are some of my hopes, dreams, and wishes for you in the

years to come: _____

_____

_____

_____

_____

_____

[Father] Here are some things I'd like you to know about how

I feel now: _____

_____

_____

_____

_____

Here are some of my hopes, dreams, and wishes for you in the

years to come: _____

_____

_____

_____

_____

_____

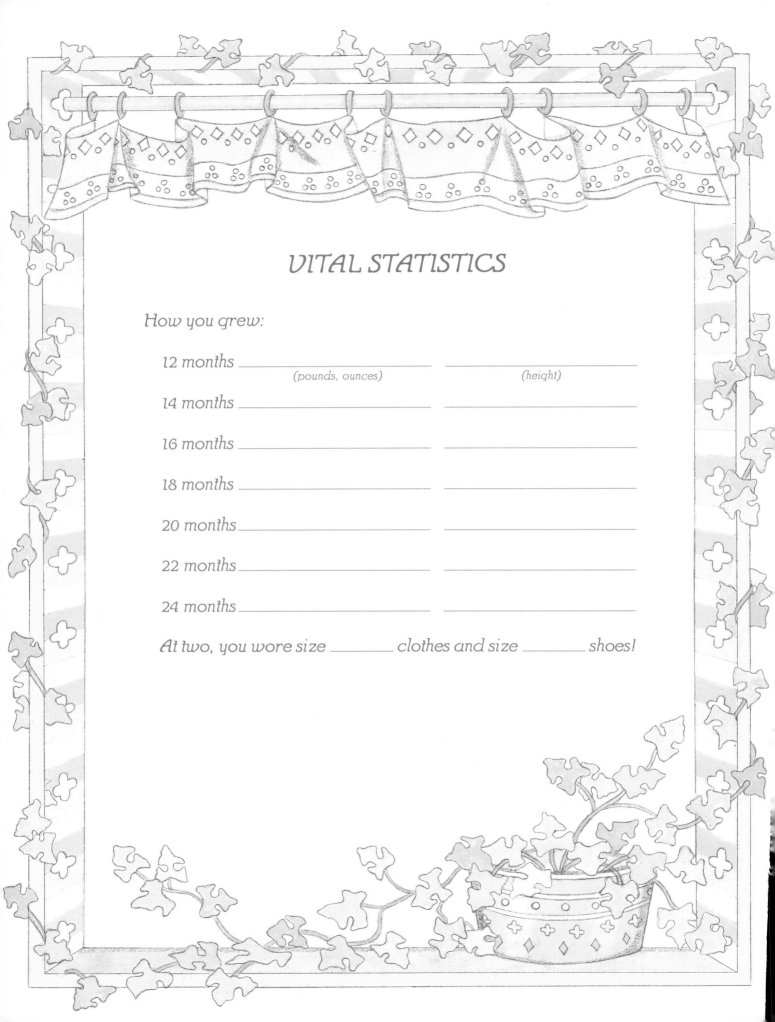

VITAL STATISTICS

How you grew:

12 months _____ _____
                  (pounds, ounces)   *(height)*

14 months _____ _____

16 months _____ _____

18 months _____ _____

20 months _____ _____

22 months _____ _____

24 months _____ _____

At two, you wore size _____ clothes and size _____ shoes!